SHADOW WORK
Journal

This journal belongs to:

Welcome...

As you hold this journal in your hands, you are embarking on a remarkable journey, a journey that will lead you to the depths of your soul, guiding you through the shadows of your past towards a brighter, more empowered future.

This journal is more than just a book; it is a trusted companion on your path to healing, understanding, and personal growth. Within these pages, you will find the tools and guidance to explore the hidden corners of your heart, to nurture your inner child, and to illuminate the shadows that have shaped your life.

You are not alone on this journey. Countless individuals have walked similar paths, and their stories of transformation and resilience inspire the creation of this journal. It is our hope that, through these pages, you will discover the strength within yourself to heal, to grow, and to reclaim your authentic self.

Here, you will find profound journal prompts to spark introspection, nurturing exercises to comfort your inner child, affirmations to strengthen your spirit, and wisdom to guide you through the process of shadow work. You will gain insight into the profound healing potential that lies within you.

Remember, healing is not linear, and there is no rush or destination. Each page you fill, every insight you gain, and every affirmation you embrace is a step forward on your unique and beautiful journey. Be patient with yourself, and always remember that your shadows do not define you, they are simply pieces of the intricate mosaic that is your life.

As you begin this sacred journey of self-discovery and healing, we invite you to embrace your shadows with love, compassion, and courage. You are deserving of every ounce of healing and growth that awaits you.

May these pages be a safe haven for your thoughts, emotions, and revelations. May they serve as a reminder that your story is important, your healing is vital, and your growth is profound.

With an open heart and boundless hope, we welcome you to this journal.

With all my love and support.

"Everyone carries a shadow, and the less it is embodied in the individual's conscious life, the blacker and denser it is."

CARL JUNG

"Within the depths of your inner child's heart lies the key to healing your past wounds and unlocking the door to a brighter future.

Embrace your shadows, for in their transformation, you discover the light of your true self."

INTRODUCTION TO SHADOW WORK:
Unveiling the Hidden Self

Within each of us lies a realm of thoughts, emotions, and experiences that we may have tucked away in the depths of our consciousness, our shadows. These shadows are aspects of ourselves that we have deemed unacceptable, painful, or uncomfortable. They stem from past wounds, unmet needs, or societal conditioning.

Shadow work is the transformative process of delving into these hidden corners of our psyche with compassion and curiosity. It's the courageous act of shining a light on the aspects of ourselves we'd rather ignore, deny, or disown. This process allows us to confront, acknowledge, and ultimately integrate these shadow aspects into our conscious awareness.

The significance of shadow work lies in its power to facilitate profound healing and personal growth. Here's why it matters:

1. **Self-Awareness:** Shadow work invites us to explore our inner landscapes with honesty. By acknowledging our shadows, we gain a deeper understanding of our fears, insecurities, and emotional triggers.

2. **Healing:** Many of our shadows are rooted in past traumas or unmet childhood needs. By confronting these wounds, we can begin the process of healing and release the emotional burdens that have held us back.

3. **Self-Acceptance:** Shadow work teaches us self-compassion. It helps us realize that our shadows are not flaws, but rather parts of our humanity. As we accept these aspects of ourselves, we can embrace our wholeness.

4. **Personal Growth:** Through shadow work, we unearth hidden strengths, talents, and resilience. By integrating our shadows, we can tap into our full potential and experience personal growth on a profound level.

5. **Improved Relationships:** As we become more aware of our shadows and how they affect our behavior, we can relate to others with greater empathy and understanding. This can lead to healthier and more fulfilling relationships.

6. **Authenticity:** Shadow work encourages us to live authentically. By shedding the masks and facades we've built to hide our shadows, we can show up as our true selves in all aspects of life.

In this journal, I invite you to embark on your own journey of shadow work. With the guidance of introspective prompts, nurturing exercises, affirmations, and inspirational wisdom, you will have the tools you need to delve deep into your shadows, embrace your inner child, and pave the way for healing and personal growth. Remember, it's a journey of self-discovery, and every step you take is a step towards a brighter, more authentic you.

"The wound is the place where the Light enters you."
RUMI

THE INNER CHILD

"Embracing and healing your inner child is like mending the wings of a wounded bird, allowing it to soar once more in the boundless sky of self-discovery and inner freedom."

THE INNER CHILD

Deep within each of us resides the essence of our inner child, a precious, vulnerable, and authentic aspect of ourselves that carries the memories, emotions, and experiences of our early years. The inner child represents the innocence, curiosity, and unbridled joy that we often lose touch with as we navigate the challenges and responsibilities of adulthood.

What is the Inner Child?

The inner child is the part of us that holds the wounds and unmet needs from our formative years. It encompasses the emotional responses, beliefs, and patterns of behavior that were shaped during childhood. These experiences, whether positive or painful, continue to influence our adult lives, often without our conscious awareness.

The Importance of Healing Your Inner Child

Healing your inner child is a transformative journey of self-discovery and self-compassion. It's a process of acknowledging, comforting, and nurturing the wounded parts of yourself. By doing so, you unlock the potential for profound healing and personal growth. Here's why it matters:

1. **Emotional Liberation:** Healing your inner child allows you to release the emotional baggage carried from the past. You can free yourself from patterns of fear, shame, and insecurity that may have held you back.

2. **Improved Relationships:** As you heal, you gain greater insight into your emotional triggers and responses. This awareness can lead to healthier and more fulfilling relationships with others

3. **Self-Compassion:** Self-compassion is the foundation of inner child healing. When you treat your inner child with love and understanding, you learn to extend that same compassion to your adult self.

4. **Authenticity:** Reconnecting with your inner child helps you rediscover your authenticity. You can shed the masks and facades that may have masked your true self, allowing you to show up more genuinely in your life.

5. **Personal Growth:** The journey of healing your inner child often reveals untapped potential, creativity, and resilience. It paves the way for personal growth and self-empowerment.

In the pages that follow, you'll find a series of prompts designed to guide you through the process of healing your inner child. Each prompt is an invitation to explore, reflect, and nurture the part of you that longs for healing and wholeness. Through this journey, may you rediscover the radiant spirit of your inner child and embark on a path of self-discovery, self-love, and transformation.

> *"Our inner child is still within us; not just a memory, but a living, breathing part of ourselves."*
>
> **THICH NHAT HANH**

Reflections

Think of a childhood memory that stirs strong emotions.
What feelings come up? How can you provide comfort and
understanding to your inner child regarding these emotions?

Reflections

Imagine your inner child as a younger version of yourself.
Write a loving letter, offering understanding and support for
any past difficulties. What comforting words would you
share to help your inner child feel safe and valued?

Reflections

Close your eyes and visualize a moment from your childhood when you felt happy and carefree. Describe this memory in detail. How did it make you feel? What activities or people were involved? Reflect on how you can bring some of that childlike joy and innocence into your adult life.

Reflect on the emotional needs you may not have received as a child. What were some of these unmet needs, such as love, validation, or safety? How have they affected your adult life and relationships? Write a letter of understanding and compassion to your inner child, acknowledging these needs and promising to provide them now.

Reflections

Imagine yourself as a loving and nurturing parent to your inner child. What would you say to comfort and support your inner child during times of distress or sadness? Write a letter from your inner parent to your inner child, offering guidance and reassurance.

Reflections

Identify a specific childhood wound or painful memory that still affects you today. Describe the situation, your emotions at the time, and how it has shaped your beliefs and behaviors as an adult. Explore how you can begin the process of healing and releasing this wound.

Reflections

Remember the activities or hobbies you enjoyed as a child. Is there something you used to love but have abandoned as an adult? Reconnect with that childlike sense of playfulness. Write about how engaging in these activities can nourish your inner child and bring joy into your life.

Reflections

Reflect on any resentment, anger, or blame you may hold towards your caregivers or others who may have contributed to your childhood wounds. Write a letter of forgiveness, whether or not you plan to share it. Let go of the emotional burdens that no longer serve you.

Reflections

Explore self-care practices that resonate with your inner child. What activities or rituals make you feel safe, loved, and cared for? Commit to integrating these self-care practices into your daily life to nurture your inner child.

Reflections

Imagine your healed inner child and your future self coming together to work as a team. What goals, dreams, or aspirations do you both have? How can you support each other in achieving them? Write a joint letter from your inner child and your future self, outlining your shared vision and intentions.

Notes

Notes

INNER PARENTING

"Cultivate your Inner Parent, a loving guardian within your soul who cradles your inner child, whispers words of self-compassion, and guides you toward healing and self-empowerment."

THE INNER PARENT

Welcome to the section of your journal where we explore the concept of the Inner Parent, a loving, caring presence within you that plays a vital role in your healing journey.

What is the Inner Parent?

The Inner Parent is like a nurturing caregiver residing within your psyche. It's the part of you that offers compassion, guidance, and support, especially to your inner child. This concept allows you to become your own source of love and comfort, bridging the gaps left by any neglect or pain you experienced in your past.

How Does It Relate to Your Healing Journey?

In the context of this journal, the Inner Parent concept is essential because it helps you create an internal space of safety and nurturing. This presence is here to heal and care for your inner child—the part of you that may have been wounded or neglected in your early years.

Practical Exercises:

1. **Letter from Your Inner Parent:** Take a moment to imagine your Inner Parent as a wise, loving presence. Write a letter from your Inner Parent to your Inner Child. Offer words of comfort, understanding, and encouragement. What would your Inner Parent say to help your Inner Child feel safe, valued, and loved?

2. **Visualization:** Close your eyes and visualize your Inner Parent embracing your Inner Child with warmth and tenderness. Imagine this nurturing presence soothing any emotional wounds and filling your inner space with love and care.

3. **Self-Compassion Journaling:** Whenever you encounter moments of self-criticism or inner turmoil, pause and write a journal entry from the perspective of your Inner Parent. How would your Inner Parent respond to your feelings with kindness and empathy?

By exploring the Inner Parent concept through these exercises, you'll enhance your ability to provide self-compassion, comfort, and support on your healing journey. This inner nurturing presence complements the exploration of your inner child and empowers you to become your own source of emotional healing and guidance.

> *"It's only by confronting the darkness in ourselves that we can illuminate the world around us."*
>
> **UNKNOWN**

Reflections

Imagine your Inner Parent as a loving, nurturing presence within you. Describe this inner figure in detail. How does your Inner Parent communicate with your inner child? What soothing words or actions does your Inner Parent offer in times of distress?

Reflections

Reflect on a recent situation where you felt self-criticism or self-doubt. Write a letter from your Inner Parent to your adult self, offering words of self-compassion and understanding. How does this nurturing presence help you navigate moments of self-judgment?

Reflections

Consider a specific childhood memory that still carries emotional weight for you. Write a letter from your Inner Parent to your Inner Child in that memory. How would your Inner Parent provide comfort and support to your younger self in that situation?

Reflections

Reflect on a recent experience where you needed to set healthy boundaries in your life. Describe how your Inner Parent guided you through this process. How did this inner nurturing presence help you assert your needs with love and compassion?

Reflections

Explore any past experiences of rejection or abandonment that may still affect you. Write a dialogue between your Inner Parent and your wounded Inner Child, allowing your Inner Parent to offer reassurance, love, and healing guidance.

Reflections

Recall a time when you doubted your abilities or decisions. How can your Inner Parent help you build self-trust and confidence? Write a letter from your Inner Parent, highlighting your strengths and encouraging trust in your choices.

Reflections

Reflect on any unresolved conflicts or grievances from your past. How can your Inner Parent guide you in the process of forgiveness, both for yourself and others? Write about the healing potential of forgiveness under your Inner Parent's gentle guidance.

Reflections

Create a daily or weekly inner parenting ritual. Describe the specific actions or affirmations you'll engage in to connect with and nurture your inner child. How will this ritual promote healing and emotional well-being in your life?

Reflections

Think about times when you've sought validation or approval from others. How can your Inner Parent help you learn to validate yourself? Write about the role your Inner Parent plays in guiding you toward self-acceptance and self-validation.

Reflections

Reflect on any feelings of abandonment or neglect from your past. How does your Inner Parent provide comfort and reassurance to your inner child who may still carry these wounds? Write a letter from your Inner Parent to your Inner Child, addressing these feelings and offering a sense of safety and belonging.

Notes

Notes

GUIDED EXERCISES

Here are some guided exercises to help you write a letter from your Inner Parent to your inner Child:

Exercise 1: Letter of Comfort and Reassurance

- Find a quiet and comfortable space where you can focus on your inner dialogue.

- Imagine your Inner Parent as a loving, wise presence within you. Visualize this nurturing figure offering warmth and reassurance to your Inner Child.

- Begin your letter with a loving salutation. For example, "My Dearest Inner Child," or any other term of endearment that feels right for you.

- In your letter, acknowledge any pain or struggles your Inner Child may have experienced. Validate these feelings with compassion.

- Offer words of comfort, understanding, and support. Share the wisdom and love that your Inner Parent holds.

- Encourage your Inner Child to express their emotions and needs without judgment. Let them know that they are safe and cherished.

- Close the letter with a heartfelt message of love and a promise of continued support and guidance from your Inner Parent.

Exercise 2: Future Nurturing

- Reflect on a specific challenge or fear you are currently facing in your adult life.
- Tap into your Inner Parent's wisdom and nurturing presence.
- Write a letter from your Inner Parent to your adult self, addressing the current challenge. Begin with a reassuring greeting.
- Offer guidance, comfort, and encouragement to your adult self, just as you would to your Inner Child. Imagine your Inner Parent providing solutions or offering a comforting perspective on the situation.
- Emphasize the importance of self-compassion and self-care in navigating this challenge.
- Close the letter with a reminder that your Inner Parent is always there to support and guide you through life's ups and downs.

Exercise 3: Gratitude and Encouragement

- Reflect on your personal growth and healing journey so far.
- Visualize your Inner Parent celebrating your progress and growth.
- Begin your letter by expressing gratitude to your Inner Child for their resilience and courage throughout your life.
- Share the pride and love your Inner Parent feels for your journey. Acknowledge the steps you've taken to heal and grow.
- Offer words of encouragement and support for the continued exploration of your inner world and the path ahead.
- Close the letter with a loving affirmation of your worthiness and the enduring connection between your Inner Parent and Inner Child.

Positive Affirmations

Here are a list of affirmations you can use on a daily basis.

- I am worthy of love, happiness, and fulfillment.

- I trust in the journey of my life and embrace every step.

- I am resilient, and I can overcome any challenge that comes my way.

- I am in control of my thoughts, and I choose positivity and optimism.

- I deserve abundance in all aspects of my life.

- I am constantly growing and evolving into the best version of myself.

- I am capable, confident, and equipped to handle whatever the day brings.

- I am surrounded by love and support from those who care about me.

- I am grateful for the opportunities that come my way.

- I release all negative energy and embrace inner peace and tranquility.

- I trust my intuition and make choices that align with my true self.

- I am a source of inspiration and positivity for others.

- I am deserving of success, and I achieve my goals with determination.

- I forgive myself for past mistakes and move forward with grace.

- I am a magnet for joy, and I attract positivity into my life.

Breathing Exercises

Here are some daily breathing exercises you can incorporate in your daily life and practice. They can be a valuable addition for managing stress, promoting mindfulness, and supporting the healing journey.

Incorporating breathing exercises into your daily life can be a valuable addition for managing stress, promoting mindfulness, and supporting the healing journey. Here are a few breathing exercises that can be included:

Breathing Exercise 1: Calming Breath

Begin your journaling session with this calming breath exercise to center yourself and create a peaceful, focused state of mind.

- Find a quiet, comfortable space to sit or lie down.

- Close your eyes and take a deep breath in through your nose, counting to four as you inhale.

- Hold your breath for a count of four.

- Exhale slowly and completely through your mouth, counting to six as you release the breath.

- Repeat this process for a few cycles, allowing each breath to calm your mind and body.

- As you journal, maintain this slow, rhythmic breathing to promote relaxation and presence.

Breathing Exercise 2: Box Breathing for Emotional Regulation

This exercise can help regulate emotions and reduce stress as you work through challenging thoughts or memories in your journal.

- Visualize a square shape in your mind. Each side of the square represents a part of the breath cycle (inhale, hold, exhale, hold).

- Inhale for a count of four, imagining yourself tracing the first side of the square.

- Hold your breath for a count of four, as if you're moving along the second side of the square.

- Exhale for a count of four, following the third side of the square.

- Hold your breath again for a count of four, completing the square.

- Repeat this process several times to regulate your emotions and maintain a sense of calm while journaling about potentially distressing topics.

Breathing Exercise 3: Body Scan and Breath Awareness
Use this exercise to bring mindfulness to your body and connect with your inner sensations.

- Sit or lie down comfortably, closing your eyes.

- Take a few deep breaths to settle into the moment.

- Begin to mentally scan your body from head to toe. As you do, notice any areas of tension, discomfort, or relaxation.

- With each inhale, imagine sending healing, relaxing energy to any tense areas, and with each exhale, release any tension or stress.

- Continue to scan your body, directing your breath and intention to any areas that need attention.

- As you journal, maintain this connection to your breath and body, allowing it to anchor you in the present moment.

PERSONAL GROWTH & DEVELOPMENT

"Personal growth and development are the keys to unlocking the boundless potential that resides within you. Embrace the journey, for it is the path to becoming the fullest expression of yourself."

PERSONAL GROWTH

Personal growth and development encompass the deliberate and transformative process of evolving emotionally, psychologically, and spiritually. It involves making conscious choices to heal past wounds, nurture your inner child, and become a more authentic, resilient, and fulfilled individual.

1. Healing Childhood Trauma: Personal growth in this context often begins with acknowledging and addressing the impacts of childhood trauma. It involves facing the emotional scars and unmet needs from the past and taking intentional steps to heal and release them. This healing process may include therapy, self-reflection, self-compassion, and nurturing exercises that help you reconnect with your inner child.

2. Nurturing the Inner Child: Central to personal growth in the context of healing is the concept of nurturing your inner child. This involves providing the care, love, and understanding that may have been lacking during your formative years. As you nurture your inner child, you create a foundation of self-compassion, self-acceptance, and self-love. This inner nurturing enables you to heal, grow, and live authentically.

Shadow Work in Personal Growth

Shadow work plays a pivotal role in the larger context of personal growth, especially when healing childhood trauma and nurturing the inner child. Here's how shadow work fits into the journey of personal growth:

1. **Self-Exploration:** Shadow work encourages deep self-exploration by inviting you to delve into the hidden aspects of your psyche. It enables you to uncover suppressed emotions, negative beliefs, and unresolved issues that may be hindering your personal growth.

2. **Healing and Integration:** Shadow work allows you to heal past wounds and integrate disowned or rejected parts of yourself. As you confront and embrace your shadow aspects, you gain a greater sense of wholeness and self-acceptance.

3. **Self-Awareness:** Through shadow work, you develop heightened self-awareness. This awareness is essential for personal growth as it helps you identify self-limiting patterns, beliefs, and behaviors that need to be transformed.

4. **Emotional Resilience:** Shadow work fosters emotional resilience by teaching you to face challenging emotions with courage and compassion. This resilience is a key component of personal growth, enabling you to navigate life's ups and downs with greater equanimity.

5. **Authenticity:** Ultimately, shadow work facilitates the journey toward authenticity. By embracing your shadow aspects and nurturing your inner child, you create a solid foundation for living in alignment with your true self, which is a central goal of personal growth.

In summary, personal growth and development in the context of healing childhood trauma and nurturing the inner child involve a deliberate journey of healing, self-discovery, and transformation. Shadow work, as an integral part of this process, empowers you to uncover, heal, and integrate the hidden aspects of your psyche, paving the way for a more authentic, resilient, and fulfilled life.

Reflections

Reflect on your healing journey so far. What progress have you made, and what challenges have you encountered?

Reflections

Consider a past painful experience. What valuable lessons or insights have you gained from it that contribute to your personal growth?

Reflections

What does personal growth mean to you, and
how does it relate to your healing process?

Reflections

How have you changed as a result of your healing journey?
What positive changes do you hope to see in your future self?

Reflections

Describe how self-compassion plays a role in your healing and personal growth. What self-compassion practices do you use regularly?

Reflections

Write about your experiences with forgiveness
on your healing journey. How has forgiveness
been a catalyst for your personal growth?

Reflections

Identify any limiting beliefs that have held you back in your healing process. How can you challenge and transform these beliefs to support your growth?

Reflections

Recall a challenging moment during your healing journey.
How did you demonstrate resilience, and what did you
learn from that experience?

Reflections

List three personal growth goals you'd like to
achieve in the next year. How will these goals
contribute to your overall healing?

Reflections

How has embracing vulnerability been a catalyst
for your personal growth? Share an experience
where vulnerability led to healing.

Reflections

Who are your role models or sources of inspiration
for personal growth and healing? What qualities do
they possess that you admire?

Reflections

Write down three positive affirmations related to
your personal growth and healing. Repeat them
daily and reflect on their impact.

Reflections

Describe your current self-care routine. How does
it support your well-being and growth?

Reflections

What healthy coping strategies have you
developed on your healing journey? How do they
contribute to your personal growth?

Reflections

Share a time when you embraced a new
perspective or belief that positively impacted your
healing and growth.

Reflections

Have you sought mentorship or guidance from others in your healing and personal growth journey? Describe how it has benefited you.

Reflections

Write down three things you're grateful for in your
healing and personal growth journey. How does
gratitude influence your outlook on life?

How have you established and maintained healthy boundaries on your healing journey? How does this contribute to your personal growth?

Reflections

Share a daily ritual that sets a positive tone for
your day and supports your growth.

Reflections

Describe a setback you've encountered on your healing journey. How did you overcome it, and what did you learn from the experience?

How does adopting a growth mindset contribute to your healing process? Share an example of when a growth mindset helped you overcome a challenge.

Reflections

Reflect on the power of your self-talk. How can
you shift negative self-talk to be more supportive
of your healing and personal growth?

Reflections

What new opportunities or experiences have you
embraced as part of your healing and growth?
How have they enriched your life?

Reflections

Write a letter to yourself affirming your worthiness
of love, healing, and growth. What words of
encouragement would you offer?

Reflections

Describe your intentions for the next phase of your healing journey. How do these intentions align with your personal growth goals?

Reflections

List three achievements, no matter how small, that
you've accomplished on your healing journey. Take
a moment to celebrate them.

How can you be a positive role model for others who may be on their own healing and growth journeys?

Reflections

Share an experience where you confronted a fear
that was holding you back. How did facing this fear
contribute to your growth?

Reflections

Write a letter of gratitude to those who have supported
you on your healing journey. How have their support and
encouragement facilitated your growth?

Reflections

Take a moment to visualize your ideal self, fully healed and grown. Describe this vision and the steps you can take to move closer to it.

Notes

Notes

Notes

Notes

Self Love

Self-care is the deliberate and ongoing practice of tending to one's physical, emotional, and mental well-being. It involves prioritizing your needs, setting boundaries, and engaging in activities that promote health, relaxation, and personal growth. In the context of the healing process, self-care is not a luxury but an essential tool for recovery and growth.

The Importance of Self-Care in Healing

1. **Physical Health:** Healing from trauma or addressing inner wounds can be emotionally and physically draining. Engaging in self-care activities such as regular exercise, a balanced diet, and adequate sleep provides the physical strength and energy needed to navigate the healing journey.

2. **Emotional Regulation:** Self-care practices help regulate emotions. Trauma and inner child work can bring up intense feelings. Activities like mindfulness meditation, deep breathing exercises, or journaling provide healthy outlets for processing and managing these emotions.

3. **Stress Reduction:** Healing can be stressful, and chronic stress can hinder the recovery process. Self-care activities like yoga, meditation, or spending time in nature help reduce stress levels, promoting a sense of calm and well-being.

4. **Self-Compassion:** Healing often involves confronting painful memories and emotions. Self-care encourages self-compassion and self-kindness. Treating yourself with love and understanding, as you would a friend, fosters emotional resilience.

5. **Boundary Setting:** Setting healthy boundaries is a crucial aspect of self-care. It involves recognizing your limits and communicating them to others. In the context of healing, it allows you to protect your emotional space and focus on your well-being.

6. **Self-Reflection:** Self-care includes practices like journaling or self-reflection, which promote self-awareness. A deep understanding of your thoughts and feelings is essential for identifying areas that need healing and personal growth.

7. **Preventing Burnout:** The healing process can be intense and prolonged. Without self-care, you risk burnout, which can set back your progress. Regular self-care helps you maintain a sustainable pace in your journey.

8. **Boosting Self-Esteem:** Self-care nurtures self-esteem and self-worth. Engaging in activities that make you feel good about yourself reinforces the belief that you are deserving of healing, love, and happiness.

9. **Supporting Inner Child Work:** In the context of healing your inner child, self-care creates a safe and nurturing environment for this inner work. By treating yourself with love and care, you extend that love to your inner child, providing them with the comfort and security they need.

10. **Long-Term Sustainability:** Healing is not a destination but an ongoing process. Self-care practices that become ingrained in your daily life ensure that you can continue to nurture your well-being and personal growth long after initial wounds have healed.

SELF-CARE ACTIVITIES

Here are examples of self-care activities that you can incorporate into your healing journey:

- Practice mindfulness meditation to stay present, calm your mind, and gain clarity during the healing process.

- Write in a journal to express your thoughts, feelings, and experiences. This can help you process emotions and gain insights into your healing journey.

- Engage in deep breathing exercises to reduce stress and anxiety, promoting relaxation and emotional regulation.

- Practice self-compassion by speaking kindly to yourself, acknowledging your feelings, and treating yourself with the same love and understanding you would offer to a friend.

- Explore creative outlets such as art, writing, music, or dance to express your emotions and find solace in creativity.

- Engage in physical activities like yoga, walking, or dancing to release tension, improve mood, and enhance physical well-being.

- Establish self-care rituals such as regular baths, skincare routines, or soothing bedtime routines to pamper yourself and foster relaxation.

- Consult with a therapist, counselor, or support group to receive guidance, validation, and professional assistance in your healing journey.

- Practice setting healthy boundaries to protect your emotional space and prioritize your needs.

- Spend time in nature to gain perspective, rejuvenate your spirit, and experience a sense of peace and connection.

- Read books or articles related to healing, personal growth, and self-compassion to gain knowledge and insights that can aid your journey.

- Cultivate a gratitude practice by reflecting on the things you are thankful for, fostering a positive mindset.

- Spend quality time with friends and family who provide support, understanding, and love.

- Pay attention to your eating habits and choose nourishing foods that support your physical and emotional well-being.

- Prioritize restful sleep and engage in relaxation techniques before bedtime to ensure adequate rest and rejuvenation.

- Practice guided visualization or positive affirmations to envision your healing journey and future growth.

- Dedicate a day to pampering yourself with spa treatments, self-care rituals, and relaxation activities.

Notes

Notes

Notes

Notes

Notes

Notes

Notes

Notes

Notes

Notes

Notes

Notes

Notes

WORDS OF GRATITUDE & ENCOURAGEMENT

I want to take a moment to express my heartfelt gratitude to you. Your decision to embark on this journey of healing and personal growth is both courageous and inspiring.

You've chosen a path that requires strength, vulnerability, and self-compassion, and for that, I commend you. It takes incredible resilience to face the shadows of the past and to nurture your inner child. You are demonstrating immense love and care for yourself, and that is a remarkable testament to your inner strength.

As you move forward on this healing journey, please remember that you are not alone. You have a support system within yourself, the loving, nurturing Inner Parent you are cultivating, and you also have a community of individuals who understand and empathize with your experiences.

Embrace each step of this journey with the knowledge that you are deserving of every ounce of healing and growth that it brings. You are worthy of love, joy, and fulfillment. The challenges you face are stepping stones to a more authentic and vibrant you.

Your journal is a safe space for your thoughts, feelings, and revelations. Use it to celebrate your victories, to release your pain, and to reflect on your progress. Your story is important, and your healing is a testament to your strength.

I am genuinely happy that you've chosen to go through this transformational journey. Keep going, dear friend. You are on the path to becoming the fullest expression of yourself, and that is a beautiful and worthwhile endeavor.

FREE SKETCHES

FREE SKETCHES

FREE SKETCHES

FREE SKETCHES